SLAYING THE VIRUS VILLAIN

A 4-LESSON PROGRAM TO BE USED WITH RED BALLOONS, FLY HIGH!

BY
CINDY DEE HOLMS

ILLUSTRATED BY
GRETA BUCHART

copyright © 1997 **mar*co products, inc.**

Published by **mar*co products, inc.**
1443 Old York Road, Warminster, PA 18974
1-800-448-2197

Library of Congress Catalog Card Number: 96-079859
ISBN: 1-57543-024-X

Printed in the U.S.A.

INTRODUCTION

Slaying the Virus Villains is a series of four unique and comprehensive lessons designed to teach disease prevention skills to children in grades 1-4, through motivational stories and hands-on educational art projects.

The first lesson introduces the concept of **germs** through a funny but informative read-a-loud story called **The Virus Villains.** The story is about Victor, Viola, and Violet Virus, who visit an elementary school. This story is followed by three hands-on activities that teach good health habits and demonstrate that if children practice these habits, they contribute to their own wellness and to the wellness of others.

The second lesson introduces the ***immune system*** and is taught through an art project. Each child draws his/her body in the image of a castle and uses various arts and crafts supplies to represent his/her immune system cells acting like soldiers defending their castle from attack by slaying germ invaders.

The third lesson introduces the concept of ***communicable disease*** through a hands-on bulletin board project. It stresses the importance of protecting others from our germs when we are sick.

The fourth lesson, ***Red Balloons, Fly High!,*** is a heartwarming story of two young boys, Matt and Jake. Matt and Jake do everything together and make lots of plans, even though one of them is HIV infected. The story introduces AIDS within the context of communicable diseases more familiar to children—like colds and chicken pox—which are also caused by viruses. The story stresses that it is much harder to get AIDS than these more familiar diseases and most children will ***never*** get AIDS. It suggests innovative ways for young children to show compassion and support for sick friends. Although the child with AIDS in this story eventually dies, the loss is dealt with in a supportive and uplifting manner. (Guidelines are included to help teachers deal with questions that might arise regarding death.) The ending of the story shows how friendship and love can transcend loss.

AIDS is a fact of life for children today. They acquire information about it—whether or not we intend for them to do so—through the media, friends, and overheard conversations. The majority of children who now have AIDS were born infected with the HIV virus, because the HIV virus was passed to them through their mother's infected blood. Since the number of women of childbearing age who are contracting this disease is escalating, we, as sensitive educators and concerned parents, must introduce our young children to this information about this disease in a gentle and noncontroversial manner. ***Red Balloons, Fly High!*** and the creative, educational activities that accompany the story have been designed to meet that need.

The first three lessons can be used on their own to teach good health habits. The fourth lesson can be used on its own to teach students about HIV/AIDS or to deal with loss issues. Ideally, by teaching all four lessons in a series, educators can empower young children with skills that will teach them ***responsibility for their own health***, as well as the responsibility for the well-being of others.

LESSON 1
THE VIRUS VILLAINS

PURPOSE:

In early elementary school grades, the *germ* concept is introduced by teaching children the correct way to wash their hands. This is important because hand-to-hand contact is one of the most common ways that germs are transmitted from person to person. Listening to the read-a-loud story about Victor, Viola, and Violet Virus and their ultimate defeat by Super Soap helps children understand why they must wash their hands and teaches them the proper way to do it.

MATERIALS NEEDED:

For the students: Mural paper, crayons, markers, pencils (optional)
For the leader: Copy of **The Virus Villains** (pages 4-5), vegetable oil, cinnamon, cold water, warm water, soap

ACTIVITY:

The leader should introduce the lesson by telling the students:

> Most germs are good germs, but some germs are troublemakers. These germs can make us sick. There are several different kinds of germs that can make us sick. Some of these germs are called *viruses*. Viruses are the germs that cause us to have the "sniffles" when we catch cold, and sometimes they cause us to feel sick with a stomachache. This story is about three viruses that cause these two health problems. They are the Virus Villains: Victor, Viola, and Violet.

Read **The Virus Villains**.

Then ask the group the following questions:

- Why are the Virus Villains bad? *(They can make people sick.)*
- When should you wash your hands? *(Before you eat or touch food, after going to the bathroom, and any other acceptable answer.)*
- Why did Matt get sick? *(Matt got sick because he did not wash his hands before he ate the cupcake.)*
- Pete washed his hands, and he still got sick. Why? *(He did not use soap.)*

Have each student name a favorite activity he/she enjoys doing at school or at home. As each activity is named, ask the students if they are likely to get germs on their hands as a result of the activity. (The answer is *yes* to every activity. Emphasize to the students that germs are everywhere, and it is very important that we remember to wash our hands with warm water and soap after we play and before we eat.)

Show the students how to wash their hands. Pour a small amount of vegetable oil across the palms of your hands. Spread the oil around by rubbing the hands together. Shake a little ground cinnamon on each hand to represent germs. Using only cold water, try to wash the oil and cinnamon off. It will not work. The cinnamon will remain. Then wash your hands with warm, soapy water. The "germs" will be washed away. Explain to the students that washing with both warm water and soap are needed to wash away the germs that can make them sick.

OPTIONAL ACTIVITY:

Have the students draw a class mural illustrating good health habits. Begin by having the students name some good health habits. Some examples of good health habits are:

- Washing your hands with warm, soapy water
- Eating good, healthful food
- Brushing your teeth after meals
- Getting plenty of rest
- Exercising every day
- Visiting your doctor and dentist for regular checkups
- Getting the shots you need to protect yourself from germs

Have each student choose the health habit he/she would like to draw. Using the mural paper, crayons, markers, and pencils, have the students draw a mural showing themselves following the health habit they have selected. Display the mural in the school hallway.

THE VIRUS VILLAINS

It was a day for doing something, but the Virus Villains could not decide what they wanted to do. "I'm bored," said Viola Virus. "Me, too," said Violet Virus.

Violet and Viola Virus looked to Victor, hoping he would think of something for them to do. Victor Virus was Violet and Viola's older cousin, and he usually had pretty good ideas. "I've got it!" said Victor. "This is a good day to make people sick! Let's go over to Learn-A-Lot Elementary School. There are lots of boys and girls there, and I bet they don't wash their hands after they play or before eating a snack. We can get on their hands and sneak inside of their bodies when they put their fingers in their mouths." Violet and Viola jumped up and down. "Great idea!" they shouted together. And off the three Virus Villains went to Learn-A-Lot Elementary School.

Victor was the first of the Virus Villains to spot two boys. Matt and Pete were tossing a football to each other. Victor looked at Viola and said, "Here's your chance to cause some trouble. Float down onto Matt's hand." Viola looked scared. "Wait, Victor," she cried, "What if he sees me?" "Don't worry about that, Viola," Victor answered. "We're so small that we're invisible to people. They can't see us!" Viola listened to her older cousin and landed on Matt's hand. Then Victor turned to Violet and said, "You do just what Viola did, only you land on one of Pete's fingers." "Wait, Victor," said Violet. "What if other germs are already there? Maybe they won't want my company." "Don't be silly, Violet," answered Victor. "We are very, very tiny. Millions of us can fit on Pete's hand." So Violet did as she was told. When Viola and Violet both had landed, Victor said, "Just sit there and wait."

In a few minutes, the teacher called the children in from recess. It was Matt's birthday, and his mother had brought in some cupcakes and juice. This was Matt's day and he was excited. "Wash your hands, everybody, and then we'll enjoy Matt's birthday treats," said the teacher.

Super Soap sat on the sink, waiting for the kids to use him. He could get rid of the germs on their hands. All they had to do was rub him between their wet hands and rinse his suds away with warm water. It was an easy way to get rid of germs, but not everyone wanted to bother using Super Soap.

Matt was anxious to get the party started. He glanced at his hands and said, "They're not dirty. Why should I take the time to wash them? It will just make me wait longer for my party." So Matt rushed back to his desk without washing his hands. Victor Virus was thrilled. "You did it!" he told Viola. "You're on your way now. One bite of cupcake, and in you go. Enjoy your ride. Once you get inside, you can make this kid sick."

Pete didn't want to take the time to wash his hands either, but he thought he should at least run a little water over them to rinse off the dirt. He turned on the water and wet his hands a little. Super Soap shouted, "No! Stop! Wait! Use me!" But Pete was in a hurry. He quickly dried his hands and rushed back to his desk. Violet got a bit wet, but she hung on. Victor laughed and said, "You've made it now, Violet! You'll be inside of Pete and making trouble in no time."

Victor was proud of his two cousins. He had been right. Learn-A-Lot Elementary School was a great place to visit. There are lots of kids here who forget to wash their hands or who wash quickly without using Super Soap. Victor hated Super Soap. Super Soap was always trying to ruin his fun.

Victor had been so busy with Violet and Viola that he had forgotten about himself. He felt like causing some trouble, too. So he floated down onto Kelly's hand. Kelly was helping Matt give out the cupcakes. Victor said to himself, "This is going to be easy!" But just before Kelly picked up the first cupcake, her friend, Andrew, asked, "Did you remember to wash your hands?" "Oh, no! I forgot," said Kelly. She put the tray down and rushed off to the bathroom. "Oh, no! Forget it kid. You don't need to wash," shouted Victor. But Kelly had good health habits. As she ran the water over her hands, Victor saw Super Soap sitting on the sink glaring at him. "Maybe she'll only use water, and I'll just get a little wet," thought Victor. But Kelly reached for Super Soap and rubbed her hands together to make lots of suds. "Oh, no!" cried Victor. "I'm in trouble now!" With that, Kelly turned on the warm water and washed off the soap. "Bye, bye, Victor Virus," shouted Super Soap, as he watched Victor slide down Kelly's hand and down the drain. Kelly was safe. There would be no trouble for her or for any of the other kids who would eat the cupcakes that Kelly touched, as long as they had washed their hands, too.

The next day the whole class went on a field trip to the zoo. Everyone that is, except for Matt, who was home with a stomachache and Pete, who had the sniffles and had caught a nasty cold.

LESSON 2
HOW THE BODY FIGHTS GERMS

PURPOSE:

Germs can get into your body in many different ways. This lesson introduces the concept of the immune system by comparing the body to a castle and comparing the immune system cells (white blood cells) to soldiers that defend the castle.

MATERIALS NEEDED:

For the students: Copy of **My Body Fighting Germs** (page 7), scissors, glue, markers, arts-and-crafts materials (glitter, pom-poms, beads, sequins, sparkles, etc.)
For the leader: Transparency of **Your Body Is Like A Castle** (page 8), copy of **How The Body Fights Germs** (page 9), overhead projector

ACTIVITY:

The leader should introduce the lesson by telling the students:

> Our bodies are always fighting germs. There are germs in the water we drink, in the air we breathe, and in the food we eat. Most germs are harmless, but some germs are trouble-makers. These germs can cause disease. Germs that sometimes make us sick are called viruses, bacteria, fungi (plantlike germs) and one-celled animals (protozoa). These germs are so tiny that we can't see them without using a microscope. A microscope makes germs and other things look many times larger than they really are.

Put the transparency of the castle on the overhead projector. Read **How The Body Fights Germs**. As you read the story, point to the parts of the picture that relate to the story text.

Give each student a copy of **My Body Fighting Germs**, arts-and-crafts materials, glue, scissors, and markers. Tell the students that they may draw other body openings—such as a nose, sore, or cut—on their faces. After they have completed that, the students should add the body's defenses (tears, ear wax, saliva, etc.) to the picture, using an assortment of arts-and-crafts materials. Glitter may be used for tears, black pom-poms for germs, etc. Open sores on the skin can be drawn with soldiers surrounding the injuries. Students may use larger white pom-poms to represent the blood cells that are acting like soldiers defending the body against invading germs. Set a time limit for this activity. When the students have finished, display the pictures throughout the room.

MY BODY FIGHTING GERMS

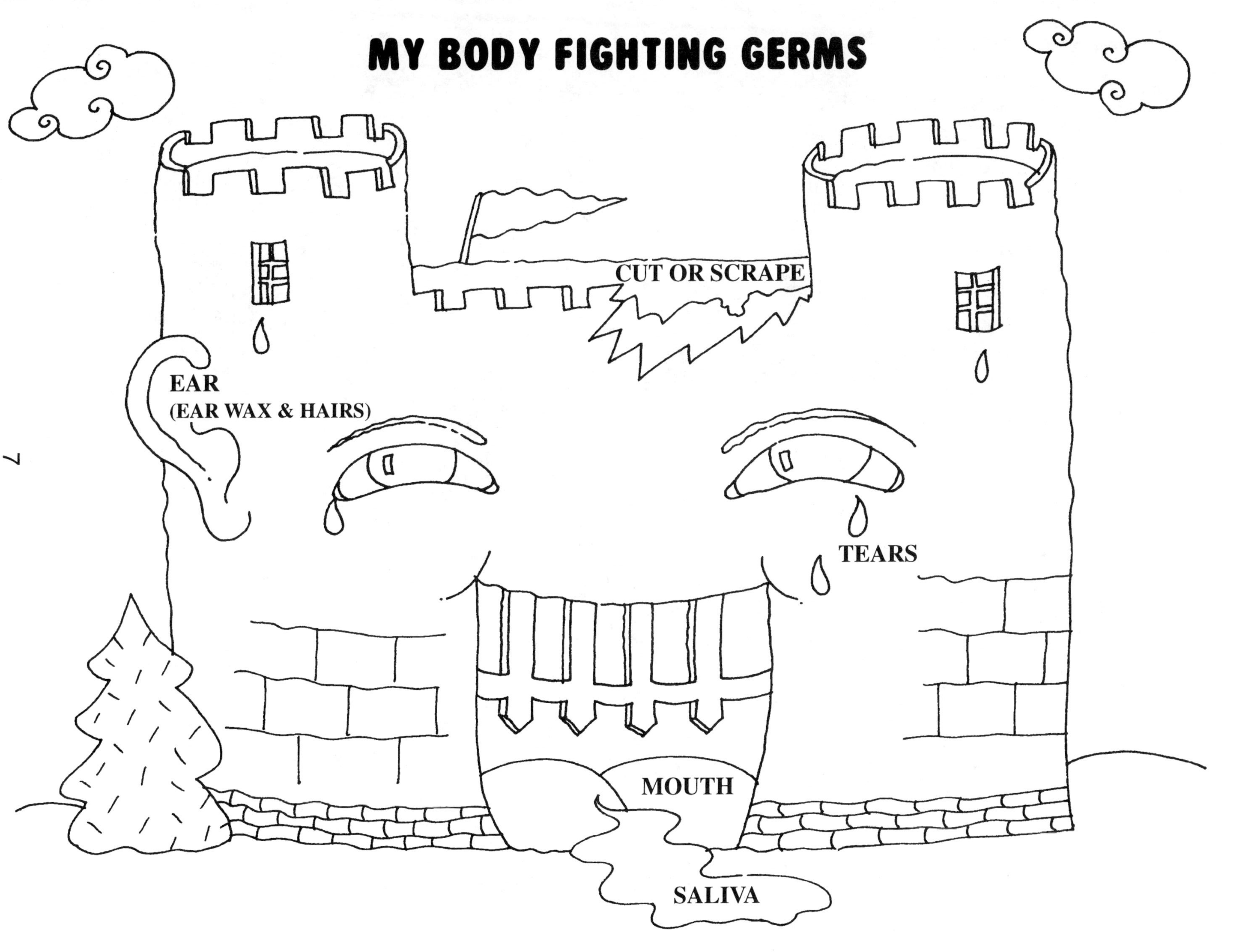

YOUR BODY IS LIKE A CASTLE

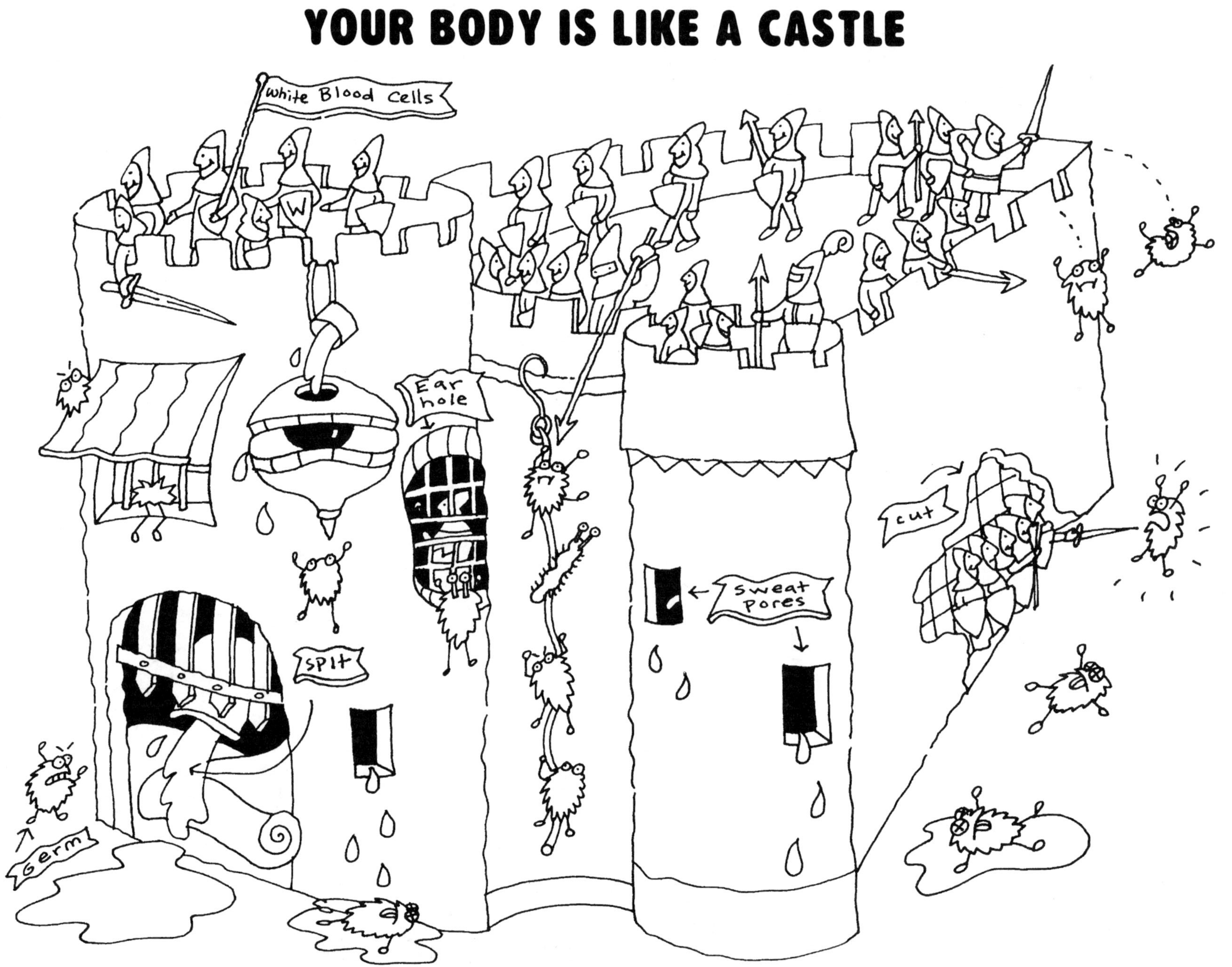

HOW THE BODY FIGHTS GERMS 

Our bodies have lots of ways to defend us against trouble-making germs. First of all, our skin is a strong barrier. Our skin protects our bodies the same way a wall protects a castle. (Point to the wall.) Germs cannot get through our skin unless there is a cut in it. Even if we do cut or scrape our skin, white blood cells that act like soldiers guarding a castle wall (Point to the soldiers guarding the wall by the cut.) will rush to the spot where our skin is injured and try to kill the germs that are trying to get inside us. These white blood cells (soldiers) are called the body's immune system.

Germs also try to get into our bodies through other openings. Think of the openings that you have on your face. First, look at your eyes. They have openings, but they are well-guarded against germ attack by tears. Tears kill germs. When you blink, tears wash your eyes. (Point to the eye on the transparency and show the tears washing away germs.)

Germs also try to get into your nose, but sticky hairs inside your nose trap germs in the air you breathe. These hairs keep the germs from getting into your body. Sometimes, germs annoy your nose so much, you sneeze. When you sneeze, your body gets rid of germs. But unless you cover your nose and mouth and wash your hands with warm water and soap right after you sneeze, your germs can make someone else sick.

Your mouth is a favorite way for germs to get into your body. That's why it's important to wash your hands with warm, soapy water before you eat. If you don't, the germs that are on your hands will find it easy to get into your body. Luckily, most germs get swallowed with our saliva (Point to the spit and germs.) and end up in the stomach, where the stomach juices that help us digest food kill them.

Your ears have openings, too. Ear wax protects your ears from germs. Germs are trapped in the sticky stuff. (Point to the ear hole.) Ear wax works the same way as the sticky hairs in your nose, trapping germs and keeping them from getting inside your body.

It is also very important to wash your whole body. There are tiny holes in your skin called pores. Pores let out sweat. Clean sweat kills germs, but old sweat traps dirt. That is why it is important to make sure that you wash off the old sweat. (Point to the sweat pores.)

Even though you have all these defenses, sometimes trouble-making germs can still get into your body. When they do, your body's white blood cells go to work. Your body has millions of these immune system cells, and they act like soldiers to defend you against a germ attack. Most of the time, your white blood cells kill the invading germs so that you can stay healthy. Sometimes, though, the invading germs are so strong that they are able to make you sick for awhile. That's what happens when you have a cold or the chicken pox. Each of these two illnesses is caused by a germ called a virus. When you get either of these illnesses, it means that your white blood cells didn't kill all the germs right away. But don't worry! Your white blood cells will keep on fighting these viruses until your immune system soldiers win the battle and you get well. While the white blood cells are fighting these viruses, a doctor may prescribe medicine for you to take to help you feel better.

LESSON 3
COMMUNICABLE DISEASES

PURPOSE:

To introduce the concept of communicable disease (when germs can spread from one person to another) within the context of familiar communicable diseases like chicken pox and the common cold.

MATERIALS NEEDED:

For the students: None
For the leader: A spray bottle filled with colored water, a box of tissues, a large cut-out figure of a boy and a large cut-out figure of a girl to be placed on the bulletin board, names of several communicable and noncommunicable diseases written on separate 3" x 5" cards, yarn

ACTIVITY:

The leader should ask the following questions:

- Has anyone ever had chicken pox? *(Allow time for answers. Continue, directing the questions to those students who responded positively.)*
- What did you look like when you had chicken pox? *(Covered with raised bumps or blisters.)*
- Did anyone else in your family have chicken pox right before, at the same time, or right after you did? *(If any of the students answer "yes," explain that sisters and brothers often get this disease around the same time because this disease can be spread from one person to another. It is a disease that can be caught. It is caused by a virus which is breathed into the air by a person infected with it. You can breathe the virus in from the air if you are playing with or living with a person who has chicken pox.)*
- Has anyone ever had a cold? *(Allow time for answers.)*
- What did you look like and sound like when you had a cold? *(Runny nose, coughing and sneezing, or any other acceptable answer.)*
- What did you feel like when you had a cold? *(Hard to breathe, earache, sore throat, fever, sleepiness.)*
- Did anyone else in your family or any of your close friends have a cold around the same time you did? *(If any of the students answer "yes," explain that, like chicken pox, you can "catch" a cold from someone else. This is because a cold is caused by a virus that lives in tiny droplets of water that come out of a person's mouth when he/she coughs or sneezes. If you breathe this cold virus into your own body, it will make you sick with a cold, too.)*
- *Note:* Tell the students that fewer children are getting chicken pox because doctors now have a vaccine. When the doctor injects a young child with the vaccine, it protects the child from getting chicken pox.

Conduct the following experiment:

Show the students the spray bottle filled with colored water. Ask some of the students to stand about a foot away from the bottle, each holding a tissue in the air. Ask some other students to stand about two feet away from the bottle, each holding a tissue in the air. Spray the colored water onto the tissues the students are holding. Tell the students that the bottle is like a person with a cold who is sneezing into the air. Look at all of the water droplets that mark the tissues. If this were a sneeze coming from a person with a cold, each of these droplets would contain thousands of cold viruses. When a sneezing person doesn't cover the sneeze with his or her hand or a tissue, all those viruses go out into the air for others to breathe. Cold viruses can live on surfaces where they land, but they're so small, you can't see them. If you touch those surfaces (like a pencil, door knob, or ball) and then put your hand to your mouth to eat without first washing your hands, you allow the cold viruses to go right into your body with your food.

Tell the students that another way they can "catch" a virus or other kind of germs is through body fluids, like saliva. Ask:

Why is sharing a cup or a straw with another person not a good idea? *(The other person's saliva might have germs in it. Those germs could get into your body and make you sick.)*

Tell the students that sometimes they don't feel well because of conditions that are not caused by germs. Ask:

Can you name some of these conditions? *(Broken bones, allergies, asthma, or any other acceptable answer. If stomachaches and headaches are mentioned, tell the students that both of these illnesses can be caused by germs, but they can also be caused by other factors, such as being upset or worried. Tell the students that if they are upset or worried, they should talk about their feelings and concerns with an adult whom they trust.)*

Tack the large boy and girl cut-out figures on the bulletin board. Put the 3" x 5" cards listing the communicable and noncommunicable diseases mentioned in this lesson in random order in a line under one of the figures on the bulletin board. Under the second figure and across from each 3" x 5" card, place a tack.

Then ask:

Which of the conditions listed on these cards can be passed on to another person?

As the students identify the conditions that are communicable, attach a piece of yarn to the tack holding the 3" x 5" card on which the condition is listed. Connect the other end of the yarn to the opposite tack across from the card and under the second figure.

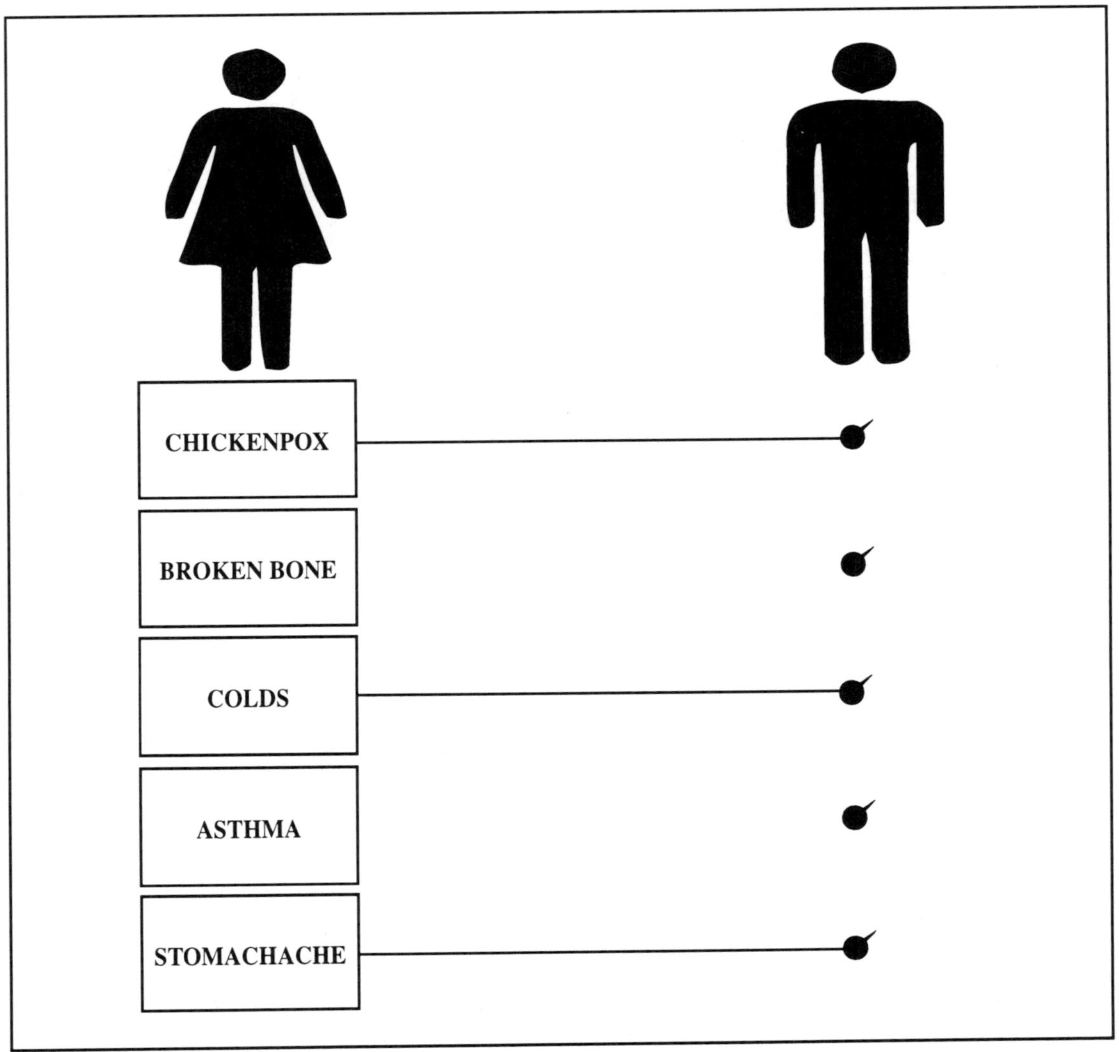

Review the modes of transmission by asking the students to name the ways each of the communicable diseases is passed between people. Their answers should include:

- Through the air—you breathe in germs
- Through surfaces where a germ has landed— like on a person's hand that then rubs an eye or a nose or puts food into the mouth
- Through body fluids like saliva—when you spit, cough, sneeze, or share a cup

Ask the students to name some ways they could prevent passing germs that cause stomachaches, colds, or chicken pox. If the answers below are not included, be sure to mention them:

- Use a tissue to cover your mouth when you cough or sneeze.
- Don't handle another person's tissue.
- Wash your hands often and always before eating.
- Don't drink out of another person's cup or straw or use his/her fork or spoon.
- When you have chicken pox, stay home from school until the doctor says you can return to class.

LESSON 4
RED BALLOONS, FLY HIGH!

PURPOSE:

To provide information about AIDS, describe what it's like to be a child who has AIDS, deal with grief issues in an uplifting and gentle manner, and suggest ways to show compassion and support for people who are sick.

Note to Teachers: Please read the following information before starting the lesson.

Transmission of HIV:
This story is directed toward early elementary school-age children, primarily 1st through 3rd or 4th grades. It does **not** include information regarding transmission of HIV through sex. Instead, it concentrates on transmission through blood between mother and child. If desired, explain that most children who have AIDS were born infected with HIV because the virus was passed to them through their mother's infected blood. The child comes into contact with that blood either before or at the time of birth. This story also provides a **Safe Play Rule** which teaches children not to touch the blood of a friend who is injured and bleeding (see last activity in Lesson #4). For most younger children, this information will be sufficient. If you wish to include information about transmitting the virus through sex or IV drug use, read the following: (Check with the school principal before using either of these explanations.)

Transmission Through Sex:
The major cause of HIV transmission among adults is through sexual contact. If you wish to address this with your class or if a child asks a question about it, you might say, "Most adults who have acquired AIDS have done so by having sex (or sexual intercourse) with someone who has AIDS or the virus that causes AIDS. AIDS is caused by a very, very, tiny germ that we can't see. When two people (who may be married) want to show their love for each other, they have sexual intercourse by getting very close to each other in a special way. If one of the people has HIV, the virus that causes AIDS, the tiny HIV virus can move from that person to the other person."

Transmission Through IV Drug Use:
The second major cause of HIV transmission in adults is IV drug use. If you want to address this issue, you might say, "When drug users share the same needle, the first person's blood gets mixed with the second person's blood. If the first person has the virus that causes AIDS in his/her blood, that virus can be passed to the second person."

If further information is needed regarding HIV/AIDS call:

The National AIDS Hotline
Centers for Disease Control
1-800-342-AIDS (English)

1-800-344-SIDA (Spanish)
The National AIDS Information Clearinghouse
1-800-458-5231

MATERIALS NEEDED:

For each student: Copy of **Playing With A Friend Who Has AIDS Won't Give You AIDS**
(page 15), pencil, markers
For the leader: The book **Red Balloons, Fly High!**

ACTIVITY:

The leader should introduce the lesson by sharing with students any of the previous information that is appropriate.

Read **Red Balloons, Fly High!**

Ask the following questions about friendship:

- Why was Matt a good friend to Jake? *(Accept any appropriate answers.)*
- What could students do to help a sick friend feel better? *(Make cards, make a mural of get-well wishes on a banner, make a get-well video and send it to the student who is sick at home)*
- What could students do to make a friend who has AIDS feel more comfortable when he/she is in school? *(Include him/her in your games, don't call him/her names, don't act as if you are afraid to play with him/her)*

Give each student a copy of **Playing With A Friend Who Has AIDS Won't Give You AIDS**,
pencil, and markers. Have the students complete the drawing. When they have finished,
discuss the meaning of the title.

Review the **Safe Play Rule**:

If a friend gets a cut or a scrape and is bleeding, don't touch his/her blood. Get an adult to
help.

Tell the students that following the **Safe Play Rule** will protect them from coming into contact
with many different kinds of germs that can be carried in blood. It will also prevent germs that
may be on their fingers from getting into a friend's open sores.

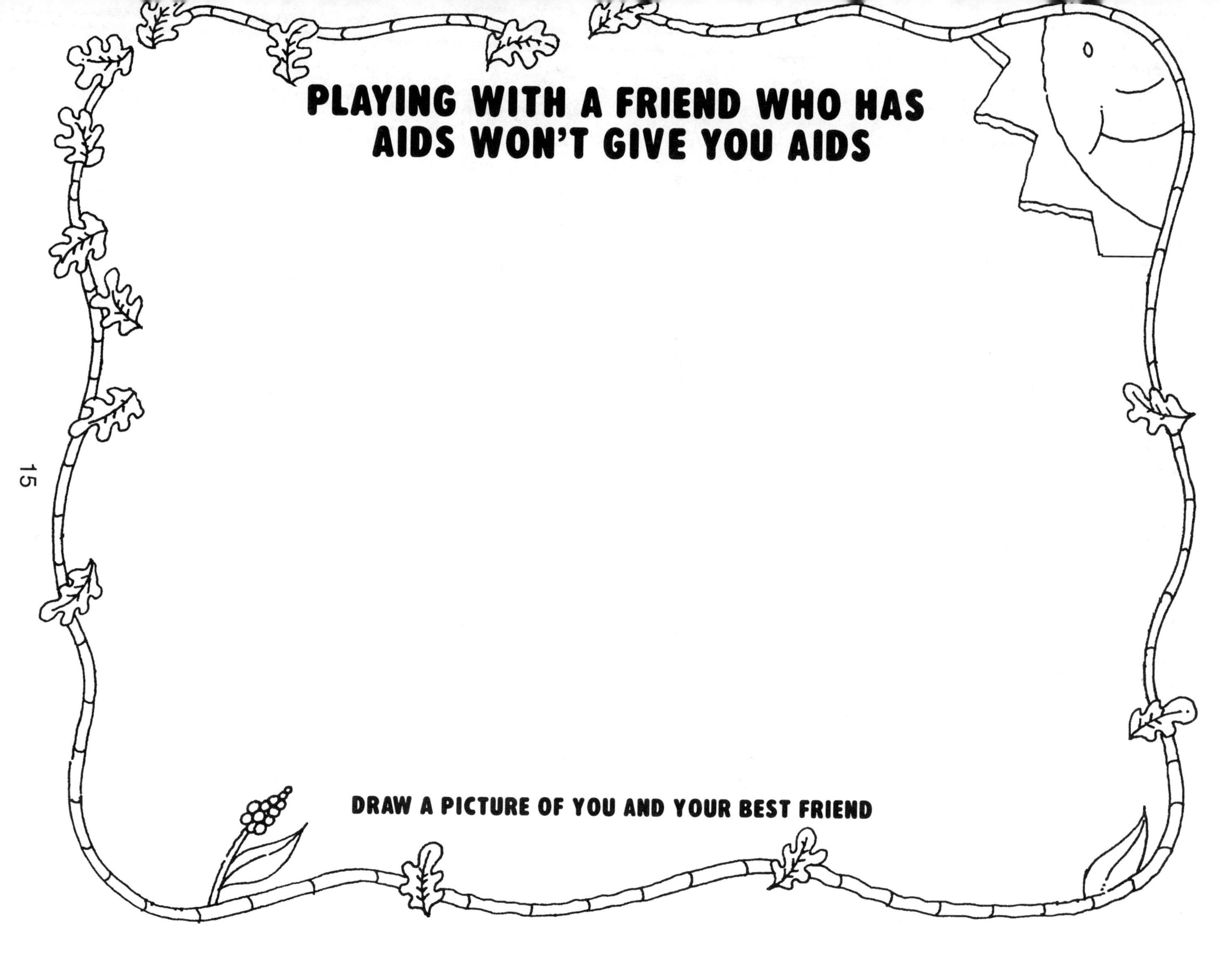

PLAYING WITH A FRIEND WHO HAS AIDS WON'T GIVE YOU AIDS
DRAW A PICTURE OF YOU AND YOUR BEST FRIEND

GUIDELINES FOR TEACHERS AND COUNSELORS FOR ANSWERING QUESTIONS REGARDING DEATH

It's important that you address the grief issue as soon as you have finished reading this book. It is unlikely that you will have a student in your class who hasn't experienced death at some level, perhaps the loss of a pet or an older relative. Even the death of a pet goldfish can cause feelings of loss. You don't need to be an expert in grief issues to help children deal with these sad feelings. Let them ask questions, and answer them as honestly and as simply as you can. If you don't have an answer to a question, let the children know that, too. Provide an environment of trust. Be a good listener.

Following are some guidelines that are developmentally based for dealing with loss issues with children between the ages of 6 and 12.

1. At the age of 6, children can begin to understand death and loss. By the age of 12, they fully understand that death means that the body stops working, the heart stops beating, breathing stops, and the brain stops functioning.

2. Children tend to be very interested in the details of death. They may ask, for example, "What will happen to Jake's body?" Remember, use simple, honest words and phrases. Be truthful without going into too much detail. You might say, "I don't know what Jake's parents decided to do with his body. Sometimes when people die, their bodies are buried in the ground. That is one choice Jake's parents could have made."

3. As the story states, it is important to gently point out that everything that lives eventually dies. Use examples from nature (leaves, birds, etc.) to help children understand this concept. Although many people believe that a person's spirit stays alive, other people have different beliefs. Be careful not to impart your own values and beliefs to the children. You may wish to emphasize that it is very unusual for children to die. Most of the time people die when they are very, very old.

4. Tell the children that when someone we love dies, it is natural for us to be sad and to hurt very much inside. This feeling is called grief. There are things we can do that will help us feel better. You might ask, "What did Matt do to help himself feel better when Jake died?" (He carried around Jake's baseball card. By carrying something that reminded him of Jake, Matt felt that Jake was close by. Sometimes it helps to keep objects that remind us of the person who died or were important to the person who died. Matt also wrote Jake a letter and sent it to him with a big red balloon. It may help to write letters to the deceased and keep them in a journal or diary.)